Oliver Morley

The food that God intends for man

Oliver Morley

The food that God intends for man

ISBN/EAN: 9783337201500

Printed in Europe, USA, Canada, Australia, Japan

Cover: Foto ©Lupo / pixelio.de

More available books at **www.hansebooks.com**

THE FOOD THAT GOD INTENDS FOR MAN.

The key to health is for man to realize how delicate his organization is.

"Therefore I say unto you take no thought for your life what ye shall eat or what ye shall drink. Is not life more than meat?" Matthew 6-26.

What Christ is to the soul this is to the body and the conditions of receiving life are alike in each, namely, to believe and put in practice.

BY

OLIVER WM. MORLEY.

WOODLAND, MICH.

INDEX.

PREFACE.

A number of years ago some authors claimed that analysis demonstrates that the human system requires certain elements to sustain its different parts; that these elements are not found in the right proportion in such articles as sugar, butter, lard. etc ; that such articles contain only what is necessary to furnish heat and fat; that the great mortality in the human race is caused by using too much heat and fat producing food to the exclusion of food that is necessary to produce muscle; that in order to get what is necessary man should use such things as lean meat, fish, the whole of wheat, beans, cheese, peas, etc., that contain the elements necessary for the muscle and brain; that it makes no difference where man gets these elements, if they are in the right proportion: that it is right to use sugar, butter, lard, etc., to produce the necessary heat and fat if lean meat, fish, the whole of wheat, cheese and articles that contain more than the requisite proportion of muscle-producing elements are used. All authors did not agree in the last clause. Some claimed that the necessary elements for the muscle could be imparted to the system by raising bread with an acid that contained it, while others claimed that it is not right to use food in a disorganized state: that (what they considered natural food) lean meat, fish, the whole of wheat, etc., should be used. As the latter claim appeared to be more reasonable, that was the one that was the most generally adopted. Practice proved both claims to be untrue. There were not so many fevers, because dispensing with an undue quantity of heat-producing food removed the cause of them; but indigestion, constipation, ulcers in the stomach, nervous diseases, etc., prevailed to a greater extent than before. What was made by escaping from one kind of disease was offset by the unusual prevalence of others, and man fell back into the old way of thinking, that to suffer more or less from disease is the inevitable consequence of being a human being.

Some later authors claim that most diseases are caused by a bacilli that is transmitted from one person to another, and that the way to prevent disease is to prevent the transmission of bacilli. Other authors claim that the bacilli is caused by disease, not the cause of it, and that the bacilli has no power to enter a healthy body that is surrounded by circumstances not calculated to engender disease and cause disease.

Some imagine that all disease is caused by sin, and in their zeal for good morals claim that all man has to do to be healthy is to keep the body in subjection and make such effort of body and mind as is known to promote health. But they are mistaken. Vast numbers who keep their bodies perfectly subjugated and pratice all the known ways of promoting health, even children who are not old enough to know evil and who cannot keep from performing physical duties because growth to them is what labor is to adults, die prematurely, while some whose lives are full of evil live to old age.

It went the rounds of the papers a few years ago that one of the most celebrated physicians of the age declared that the science of medicine is a failure, that it cannot be relied upon. It is a failure because it undertakes to cure the disease without removing the cause.

The cause of disease in man is the use of food that is not intended for nor adapted to him.

The question that comes after this statement is: How is it that man can use food that is so unadapted as to cause disease without being aware of it? The answer is: The human system is created with certain instincts, tastes and powers of assimilation, and in order to thrive must have food that agrees with them. It is impossible to determine by analysis what these instincts demand. Taste can be educated to like things that are not adapted, but the power of assimilation cannot, and there is constant trouble when it is violated. From having used this food from childhood man is unconscious of this trouble, and when it culminates in sickness he is unaware of the cause. If man dispenses with food that is unadapted until its effect is gone from the system and then uses it, its unfitness is quickly realized by the disturbance it causes. If man dispenses with food that is adapted for any length of time it does not cause disturbance when used again; on the contrary, it is more agreeable than if used every day.

The first lesson for man to learn in order to be restored to a natural state and health is, that it is possible for his system to take in and pass off sufficient unnatural food to destroy it without his being aware that he is injuring himself.

This work shows by a law of creation (nature) as unerring as the law of gravitation, what natural food is.

The natural food of man is not limited to a few tasteless or disagreeable and unnourishing things, as is the case where people go through what is commonly called a course of dieting. God has not created necessities and virtuous desires in man without creating what is necessary to satisfy them.

With due understanding and judgment exercised in the practice of this system, man's health is assured.

I am unable to describe the gratitude that I feel in realizing that God has used me as an instrument to develop these truths, which I hope are the dawning of the brightest physical era the world has ever known.

THE AUTHOR.

PART FIRST.

The law of nature, which shows the way to determine the natural food for man, is demonstrated as follows:

Fruit is one kind of food that is natural for man, and animal and vegetable food that is natural for man grows in the way of and is the counterpart of fruit.

All kinds of fruit food is either the fruit or seed of a stalk or tree, or is intended by nature to nourish a stalk when it grows; in no case is the stalk or tree used.

As meat is the animal (neither the fruit or seed of an animal,) it is not natural food.

Man's necessity for meat has long been questioned by a great many, and a great many have refrained more or less from its use; but the world at large considers it necessary to enable man to endure physically and mentally what is required; and some have given the following reasons for thinking so:

1. As man's teeth are not like animals' that eat flesh, whose teeth are set apart and sharp at the point to enable them to tear the flesh, nor like animals that eat stalks, whose teeth are close together to enable them to grind the stalks fine, it follows that man requires food that both kind of animals do. 2. Man's stomach is not large enough to hold enough other food to give him strength to endure all that is required; as meat is more concentrated than other food, it is the best. 3. It is easier digested. 4. People have lived to a very old age who have used meat all the time without having been sick. 5. According to the Bible, God gives man meat, which is evidence that it is necessary and good.

The following are answers to these reasons: 1. It is wrong to conclude that as man's teeth are unlike either kind of animals' he requires food that both kind of animals do. The correct conclusion is, as ma's teeth are unlike either kind of animal's he does not require food that either kind of animals do. If man requires food that both kind of animals do he must require stalks as one kind of animals require them. Man can chew food that is natural for him as easy as animals can chew food that is natural for them, but it is unnatural and difficult for man to chew meat. 2. God has not created the stomach incapable of holding sufficient food that he has created for it. Man has never used wholly the food intended for him, consequently he is unable to form a correct conclusion. Meat is not so concentrated and does not contain as much nourishment to the pound as the animal food that is intended for man. The main thing that is overlooked by those who reason in this way is, it is unadapted to the human system; it will not assimilate and consequently works injury. Man's undepraved taste and power of assimilation is no more like the taste and power of assimilation of dogs than he is constructed in any other way like them. The greater strength meat gives is imaginary; being unnatural, the system makes exertion to get rid of it; this causes a stimulus which is imagined to be strength. When natural food is used the difference between real and imaginary strength is manifest. If meat is not used and natural food is until the effect of meat is gone from the system, the muscles become solid and strong (they do not have the dried-up hardness that they have when meat is used) and the whole system has life and energy that it is impossible to have when meat is used. If a piece of beef-steak is eaten then it is so difficult to chew, compared with what has been used, that that alone is evidence that it is unnatural, and the derangement it causes is irrefutable evidence. If any food that is natural is dispensed with, no matter how long, it does not cause derangement when first used again; instead, it is more agreeable than if used every day. 3. It does not follow that it is better than other food because it digests quicker. On the contrary, it is better for food to be as long in digesting as nature requires, so that there shall be strength for a proper number of hours between each time of taking food. If food is digested and the strength is passed off unnaturally quick, the strength is too great on the start and too little at the end; it is better to be more even. While the digestive power of the dog is greater than that of man, the dog does not digest food that is natural for him any quicker than man digests food that is natural for him. Strong elements do not always act quickly. The digestive power of the serpent is stronger and slower than that of a dog; he digests bones. The fact that man digests meat quicker than he does food that is unquestionably natural and quicker than a dog, whose natural food it is, is evidence that it is not natural food for man. The quickness, in this case, is not evidence of strength, but weakness. 4. People have lived to a very old age without having been sick who were great drinkers, and some have lived long who were great smokers. There is no way of knowing how much longer they would have lived if they had been more temperate. Such people seldom perform hard physical labor: they use all their strength in those habits. Besides, such cases are exceptional. The strength of constitution in such cases is generally due to the non-use of meat by the ancestors. In Ireland, Germany, and other parts of the old world, the middle and poorer classes are not able to have meat, butter and sugar only occasionally, as a luxury, as they deem it; they have to sell such things to get what is more necessary. Consequently, although they do not live wholly on natural food and are not as physically perfect as they might be, they are the healthiest and strongest people in the world. The children of those who immigrate to this country, where the middle classes have all the meat and luxuries (in the way of food) they want, deteriorate and are soon far from being as healthy as their ancestors. Pugilists say there is nothing like meat. But where do they get their great muscle and power of endurance? From their ancestors in the old country, who used very little meat. Pugilists do not realize this: meat stimulates them and makes them feel strong for the time being, and they think that meat is what made them. But it is not. Their children do not have the muscle and power of endurance that they have, which they would if meat is what makes it. 5. There are two ways of answering what the Bible says: one questions the divinity of the Bible, the other sustains it. The first way is as follows: "How is it that God gives man meat for food when He knows that he is created so that it injures him and causes great mortality in the human race? How is it that Christ used meat when he knew (if he was God) that it injures man and causes the diseases that he cured. If He had been God would He not have warned man and forbade him using it? And how is it that God gives man bond men to be his possession forever? He wrote this law in the twenty-fifth chapter of Leviticus and nowhere after annulled it. On the contrary, bond men are spoken of ᴄ   ᵐwhere after that in the Bible, as something to be, of course. ᴄ d established this institution to stand forever, when it has proven to be a great curse to the human race and is done away with by every civilized nation in the world. And how is it that God gives man strong drink and wine and it is spoken of everywhere (after the fall) in the Bible as something to be used of course; especially wine, which experience has proven to be another great curse, and the best part of humanity in every part of the world is doing all they can to do away with it. God gives man these things, yet man in order to live as God desires has to make superhuman efforts to put them away. How is all this?

The other way to answer it is as follows: "If the Creator did not write the Bible how does he communicate with man? Some claim there is no Creator or God: that nature does everything. It is hard for such to tell how nature came. There is a Creator and He has not created man and made him dependent on his Creator for instruction, guidance and government without some way of communicating His desire and will to man. That way must be with the spirit; there is no sign of any other way. Then let man communicate directly with the Creator and see what he requires man to do and how he rewards and punishes him. One way to do this is to study the spirit the Creator gives to man that is the controlling power in him in his way toward animals and things over which he has control and in his way toward his fellow man. If one man tries to injure another he will tell how bad the one that he tries to injure is. The vilest of the vile are conscious that if man does wrong that it is an injury to him and man always makes use of that understanding in trying to break down those that he desires to. On the other hand if one man tries to build up another he will tell how good he is. So it is evident that sin is punishment and righteousness is reward. Is it possible for man to live so that sin will not come upon him? If a man is using a horse, and the horse does all that is required he is not punished: it is only when he is disobedient that he is punished. It must be safe to conclude that the Creator is as merciful to man as man is to his horse. What does the Creator require man to do to enable him to live so that he will not be punished? The first thing man requires of a horse is submission to his will; the horse must acknowledge man his master. There is no reason to suppose that the Creator requires less of man: the first thing is to acknowledge the Creator his master.

Man has a knowledge of good and evil and the power to choose between right and wrong. The Creator does not say which way man shall choose: He leaves it for him to choose and rewards and punishes him according to his choice. Animals have no knowledge of good and evil, nor power to choose: they do the will of man because they are obliged to. As man has this knowledge and power he must do the will of the Creator from choice, and acknowledge the Creator his master from choice. As it is impossible for man to acknowledge anything his master from choice without loving that object more than himself he must love his Creator with all his being. How does the Creator require man to feel toward his neighbor? Man desires horses to be peaceable and not agitate each other so that they can be useful to him. If any try to ilght those around them he does not want the others to fight back, but to be quiet and let him take care of the unruly ones. There is no reason to suppose that the Creator requires less of man. He requires man to love his neighbor as himself because he cannot live in peace unless he does, and if any neighbor takes it upon himself to illtreat another, that one is not to illtreat in return and destroy the usefulness of both to their Creator, but to keep his peace and maintain his relationship to his Creator and let Him take care of the disobedient one. So it is clear that the first duty of man is to love his Creator with all his being: the next is to love his neighbor as himself, and the next is not to render evil for evil. So the spirit of the Creator teaches what Christ taught. Then see the effect of Christ's teaching upon man. All the good there is in the world has come from it. See the difference between those who have had the benefit of it and those who have not. It is the forerunner of all progress. See the truth of it verified at the death of His followers. The expression in their countenance is beyond the power of man to describe; only those who have seen it have seen the most wonderful work of God. It is not seen in the countenance of all who die professing to believe in Christ, but it is seen in some, and if He is not Divine, how does it come?

Of these two ways of thinking about the Bible, which is right? There is a law that decides it, namely: There are two kinds of all created things, a good and bad. Every good thing has its opposite in a bad thing of the same kind and they are enemies. Every good plant that is useful to man has its opposite in weeds that are an abomination to man: and every good animal that is useful to man has its opposite in beasts of prey that are an abomination to man. Man is so created that he is his own enemy; he has no enemy outside of himself, and he has the power to understand between good and evil, and understands when he is an abomination to himself and injuring himself and when he is doing good to himself, and he has the power to choose for himself, so that the responsibility rests upon himself whether he shall be an abomination to himself or not. There are two spirits of which man can partake; one is good, the other is evil. If he chooses the good he is rewarded with good and is his own friend. If he chooses the evil he is rewarded with evil and is his own enemy. The world is so created that every good thing must look to something higher for deliverance from the enemies of its kind. In an even battle the bad and evil things are the strongest and will destroy the good; good plants must look to man for deliverance from weeds or they will be destroyed by them; good animals must look to man for deliverance from beasts of prey or they will be destroyed by them; the wolf is too strong for the sheep; the lion for the cow; the hawk for the chicken, etc. Man must look to something higher for deliverance from evil; in an even battle evil is strongest and will destroy him.

What is the condition upon which a higher power will deliver those that are dependent upon it from their enemies? Man deivers plants from weeds and good animals from beasts of prey because it is for his interest to do so; he needs them for his use. God cannot deliver man from evil because it is for His interest that man shall be delived from evil so that man can be useful to Him; because man possesses a knowledge of good and evil which makes it necessary for him to realize his dependence upon God and acknowledge it by asking for what he needs and desires. If God should bestow good gifts upon man without being asked, it would tempt man to look for things to come without any effort to appreciate them. It would be like a wealthy father bestowing great gifts unasked upon an ignorant and unappreciating son; which destroys him instead of building him up. It is for man to say whether he shall be delivered from evil or not.

In regard to the future life: All things are created for the purpose of being useful to and serving something above them; good plants and animals are to be useful to and serve man; man is to be useful to and serve God. God has no more use than man for what is not good. Man has no use for abominable weeds or beasts of prey: God can not use a bad man. How can God use a man who has chosen evil all his life and come to Him with no knowledge of or desire for good. Is there any more reason to expect that God can or will use such a man than there is to expect that man can or will use abominable weeds? As this is the teaching of Christ it is irrefutable evidence that He is Divine.

Then the question still is: Why does God give man these things that are so injurious?

The answer is: It is a part of the curse consequent upon the fall of man. The food given before the fall consisted of the seed of herbs and the fruit of trees. It was not until after the fall, when his desires had become depraved, that man had a craving for unnatural food and drink. The only way for him to reach physical perfection is to do away with these unnatural desires as he does away with abominable weeds and beasts of prey that infest the earth as another part of the curse.

The earth was cursed for man's sake, so that he might raise himself by his own efforts. It was or is not Christ's mission to lessen these efforts by teaching man any of the arts necessary for his physical welfare: His mission is to save the soul. He shows that neither the food used, nor the condition of the body makes any difference with the soul; there can be a perfectly healthy body with a diseased soul, or a diseased body with a perfectly healthy soul.

PART SECOND.

To trace the fruit and seed kind of animal and vegetable food out by comparing it with fruit, commence with fruit that grows like the apple. The same kind of animal food is milk, which is the fruit of an animal. The natural cause of the fruit of the tree and animal is reproduction. Generation takes place alike in trees and animals and both grow on the same principle. When the tree drops its ripened fruit the fruit is fit to use; when the animal drops its young the milk is fit to use. Each kind is intended to serve the same purpose in nature. The part used of the fruit of a tree is intended to nourish the seed that grows with it when the seed starts to grow and become a tree. The part used of the fruit of an animal is intended to nourish the young animal. The same kind of vegetable food is squashes and other things that grow in the same way. They grow on the principle of apples and the part used is intended to serve the same purpose in nature.

Thus the three kinds of food, fruit, animal and vegetable, in this class is traced, which can be called class A.

Next, take fruit that grows like the cocoanut, which has a shell and two parts of a different nature inside. The same kind of animal food is the egg of fowls. They have a shell and two parts of a different nature inside. The cocoanut and egg grow on the same principle and are intended to serve the same purpose in nature; the milk of the cocoanut is intended to nourish the meat when it starts to grow and become a tree; the yolk of the egg is intended to nourish the white when it grows to form an animal. The same kind of vegetable food is wheat: (wheat is called vegetable food here to distinguish it from fruit and animal,) and potato.

They grow on the principle that cocoanuts do. They have what may be termed a shell and two parts of a different nature inside; the inside part is intended to nourish the outside part when it grows.

Thus the three kinds of food, fruit, animal and vegetable, in this class is traced, which can be called class B.

Next take fruit that grows like chestnuts, walnuts, etc., which have a shell with one part inside. The same kind of animal food is the eggs of fish. They have what may be termed a shell with one part inside. The same kind of vegetable food is rice and corn commonly called pop-corn. They have what may be termed a shell with one part inside. Each kind is intended to serve the same purpose in nature, namely: to grow and make a tree, an animal or a stalk.

Thus the three kinds of food, fruit, animal and vegetable, in this class is traced, which can be called class C.

Next take fruit that grows like the pine-apple, which is the fruit of a stalk and the part used is intended to nourish another part, the bunch of green sprouts at the top that grows with it when it grows to bear seed from which other pine-apples can be grown. The same kind of animal food is oysters. They grow on the principle that pine-apples do and the part that should be used is intended to serve the same purpose in nature. The same kind of vegetable food is cauliflower and parsnip. They grow like the pine-apple and the part used is intended to serve the same purpose.

Thus the three kinds of food, fruit, animal and vegetable, in this class is traced, which can be called class D.

Next take fruit that grows like grapes; the same kind of animal food is honey; the same kind of vegetable food is tomato.

Thus the three kinds of food, fruit, animal and vegetable, in this class is traced, which can be called class E.

There are five classes in all, and all the food there is that has not been mentioned belongs in one of them.

It is not possible to now determine all the food that is adapted to man, but the following rule is a guide by which to tell whether any article is adapted or not. "Any article that frustrates perfect digestion when the system is able to perfectly digest food that is unquestionably natural, is not adapted."

Some vegetables are intended for animals and like some kinds of grain are too strong for the human stomach. It is no evidence that this system is not true because all things that are adapted are not now known. Neither is it necessary to wait until all things that are adapted are known before the system is demonstrated; it may be a great many years before that is found out. It is sufficient that enough is known to establish the truth of it.

PART THIRD.

The next thing is to find what part of each kind of food is suitable for man.

The part of animal and vegetable food that is suitable is the part of fruit that is suitable.

To find the part of animal and vegetable food that is suitable by comparing it with fruit, commence with class A.

The apple is composed of four parts, the seed, the core, the skin and pulp.

The fruit of the animal is composed of four parts, the young animal, the film that grows around the young animal commonly called the cleanings. what is commonly called the sour milk, and the cream.

The squash is composed of four parts, the seed, the inwards, the skin and the meat.

The seed of the apple, the young animal and the seed of the squash are intended for one purpose in nature and all are unsuitable for food. The core of the apple, the film that grows around the young animal and the inwards of the squash are intended for one purpose in nature, and all are unsuitable for food. The skin of the apple, the sour milk and the skin of the squash are intended for one purpose in nature and all are unsuitable for food. The pulp of the apple. the cream and the meat of the squash are intended for one purpose in nature and all are suitable for food.

NEXT TAKE CLASS B.

The cocoanut is composed of three parts, the shell. the meat and the milk. Eggs of fowls are composed of three parts, the shell, the white and the yolk. Wheat is composed of three parts, the bran. the middlings and the flour. The potato is composed of three parts; (these parts can be distinguished by boiling with the skin on.) The skin is one part; there is a substance next to the skin that has a greenish cast of color and a rank, strong taste

which is another part, and the center of the potato is the other.
The shell of the cocoanut, the shell of the egg. the bran of
wheat and the skin of potato are intended for one purpose in
nature and all are unsuitable for food. The meat of the cocoanut, the white of the egg, the middlings of wheat and the
greenish rank substance of potato are intended for one purpose
in nature and all are unsuitable for food. The milk of the
cocoanut, the yolk of the egg, the flour from wheat and the center of the potato are intended for one purpose in nature and all
are suitable for food.

Class B differs from class A in that the part suitable grows
inside of the part that it is intended to nourish while in class
A the part suitable grows outside of the part that it is intended
to nourish, and in class A the part that grows is a seed, but in
class B it is a substance that resembles something suitable for
food more than a seed, yet like a seed it has the power to grow.

NEXT TAKE CLASS C.

Walnuts, chestnuts, etc.. are composed of two parts, the shell
and the meat. Eggs of fish are composed of two parts, the shell.
(which differs from the shell of the nut in that it holds a great
many eggs,) and the egg. Rice and pop-corn are composed of two
parts, the shell and the kernel of rice or corn.

The shell of the nut, the shell of the fish, the shell of rice and
the husk of corn are intended for one purpose in nature and all
are unsuitable for food. The meat of the nut, the egg of the
fish and the kernel of rice or corn are intended for one purpose
in nature and all are suitable for food.

Class C differs from all other classes in that the part that
grows is suitable for food, while in all other classes that part is
not suitable.

NEXT TAKE CLASS D.

The pine-apple is composed of three parts, the skin, the bunch
of sprouts at the top and the pulp. The oyster is composed of
three parts, the shell, the juice and the solid part. The cauliflower is composed of three parts, the leaves that are outside of
the head, the stump and the head. The parsnip is composed of
three parts, the skin, the bunch of sprouts at the top and the
meat

The skin of the pine-apple, the shell of the oyster, the outside
leaves of the cauliflower and the skin of the parsnip are intended for one purpose in nature and all are unsuitable for food.

The bunch of sprouts of the pineapple, the juice of the oyster, the stump of the cauliflower and the bunch of sprouts of the parsnip are intended for one purpose in nature and all are unsuitable for food. The pulp of the pineapple, the solid part of the oyster, the head of the cauliflower and the meat of the parsnip are intended for one purpose in nature and all are suitable for food.

Class D differs from classes A and B in that the part used is intended to nourish another part that grows with it when it grows to bear seed, while in classes A and B the part used is intended to nourish the part that grows with it when it starts to grow.

NEXT TAKE CLASS E.

Grapes are composed of three parts, the skin, the seed and the pulp. Honey is composed of three parts, the comb, the young bees and the honey. Tomatoes are composed of three parts, the skin, the seed and the pulp.

The skin of grapes, the comb of honey and the skin of tomatoes are intended for one purpose in nature and all are unsuitable for food. The seed of grapes, the young bees and the seed of tomatoes are intended for one purpose in nature and all are unsuitable for food. The seed of grapes and tomatoes are eaten but do not have any ill effect because they are not digested. The pulp of grapes, the honey and the pulp of tomatoes are intended for one purpose in nature and all are suitable for food.

Class E resembles class A more than any other. It differs from class A in that there is no core around the seed. It has only three parts.

The part suitable for food in each class is as follows: In class A, the pulp of the apple, the cream and the meat of the vegetable. In class B, the milk of the nut, the yolk of the egg, the flour from wheat and the center of the potato. In class C the meat of the nut, the eggs of the fish and the kernel of rice, or corn. In class D, the pulp of the pine-apple, the solid part of the oyster, the head of the cauliflower and the meat of the root. In class E, the pulp of grapes, the honey and the pulp of tomatoes.

PART FOURTH.

Now consider the bad effect the different articles that are commonly used for food, that are left out, has on the human system.

The bad effect of meat has been demonstrated, but the question of what can be done with it if it cannot be eaten must be answered. If it was not necessary to raise any more animals than is necessary to produce milk they could be buried after they are worn out, as horses are, but it is necessary to raise steers for hides to make harness and other kinds of heavy leather for which there can be no substitute. There is nothing so light that is so strong or will endure so much, and as it is pliable and convenient to handle, it is indispensable for such purposes.

There are always correct ways to meet necessary ends. The following are some of the ways it can be used: There should be a great many more fowls in the world than there are and they are great consumers of meat, and if they have all that is necessary to enable them to produce the greatest number of eggs they will consume a great deal. And there may be a bird found that, together with fish, will produce the animal food belonging in class C. If so, they should be tamed and kept for that purpose, and they will require a great deal; and as the world grows older and wild animals that produce fur are killed off, it may be necessary to raise animals for that purpose, which will require a great deal; and it may be found necessary in manufacturing purposes; and if there is no other way, it is better to use it for manure, of which there is a dearth, than to use it for food. It is poor economy to eat anything to save it, and finally pay out a great deal more than it is worth in doctor bills, to say nothing of the lost time and distress caused by sickness.

Now consider sugar. That is simply the juice of unnatural food boiled down. It is impossible to have perfect digestion when it is used, and there is no one thing that is the cause of so much early decay and premature death.

Now consider the classes. Commencing with class A: take milk first: That is esteemed so highly that it is often used as the main food for the sick: the reasons are that it contains all the elements necessary for the human system and in the right proportion, and is, or appears to be, very palatable and soothing. Although cow's milk contains nearly the same elements as human milk, it can not be used by children before they are weaned, without trouble. If it can not be used by children without trouble when milk is their natural food, is it possible for adults to use it when no milk is natural food? When the system is out of order from the use of meat, lard, butter, (without buttermilk,) sugar, etc., milk is very palatable and soothing if used once in a while. At such times it seems as though if man was a mind to subject himself he could do no better than to make it form a good portion of his diet. But it is impossible to make it form a considerable portion of his diet without trouble, foul stomach, and constipation, the extent of which is in proportion to the amount and length of time used.

There is no doubt but the use of milk in sickness has been the cause of a great many deaths. It is often made to form the whole diet excepting a little orange, jelly, etc. Sometimes rum is used. It causes a foul stomach which is attributed to the disease: thinking there can be nothing wrong in anything apparently so harmless as milk. If the patient has strength of constitution to overcome both the disease and the effect of milk he gets well, and such cases are cited as evidence of the value of milk. If he dies he is supposed to have been destroyed by the disease alone. How can a very sick man get well on a diet that will make a well man sick?

Next take sour milk. That is not generally used to any extent. If it should be it would cause foul stomach and constipation.

Next take butter, without buttermilk, that is used mainly for the purpose of making other food palatable. It is impossible for man to use such unnatural food as fermented bread without something to make it taste more natural, so butter is used and it makes fermented bread taste a great deal more like natural food than it does without butter. But it makes bad work in the system. With fat meat, sugar and lard, it destroys the lungs, the heart, the kidneys, the urinary organs and causes fevers. See sixth and seventh verses in preface.

Next take class B. Commence with the meat of the cocoanut.

That is unpleasant to taste and hard to chew and digest and causes constipation if used to any extent.

Next take wheat. Some think the whole of wheat is better than a part because it contains all the elements necessary for the human system, and in the right proportion, and appears to be loosening. It is not possible for man to make any one article answer for him even if there are articles that, like wheat and milk, contain all the necessary elements and in the right proportion. He must use several that are intended for him, then one will make up for what the other lacks and all will be adapted. The whole of wheat has a loosening effect at first caused by the effort of the system to get rid of it, as it is unnatural, but after a while foul stomach and constipation follow, which continue as long as it is used.

Next take potato. The greenish part next to the skin is rank and disagreeable to taste and causes constipation.

Next take the white of eggs. That is cool and inviting to man when he is burnt up with fat and sugar, but it is tasteless and uninviting to the undepraved taste and causes constipation, and it is impossible to have perfect digestion when it is used. It is not liable to be used sufficiently to cause serious trouble, yet man is better off without it. There is food enough that is adapted without using any that is not.

Constipation is caused by the use of unnatural food and not by sedentary occupations as is generally supposed. Not that there is not more vigor in active out-door pursuits, but the stomach and bowels do not suffer any more from sedentary pursuits than any other part of the system, and when wholly natural food is used there is no perceptible weakness in the bowels, let the occupation be what it may.

There is no kind in class C that is unsuitable, so take class D next. The only kind in that class that is generally used that is unsuitable is the juice of the oysters. As that is about like the white of eggs in effect, what has been said of that is applicable to the juice of oysters.

There is none in class E that is generally used that is unsuitable, so the classes are finished. But there are other considerations.

Unnatural food is to a great extent the cause of the use of strong and intoxicating drinks. The food causes an unnatural thirst, which water will not quench, and something which appears to offset the effect of the food is taken instead of water.

A great many die prematurely from the use of unnatural food and intoxicating drink, but a great many more die prematurely by the use of unnatural food alone. The great mortality among children is mainly caused by the use of fermented bread and butter, without buttermilk, lard, fat meat, gravy and sugar. Children are given what they like best and as their taste is comparatively undepraved they do not like lean meat, (although lean meat is unnatural and works injury it is less injurious than fat and sugar, and after people get old enough to make it form a good portion of their diet they escape a great deal that children suffer,)so they eat what tastes more like natural food, bread and butter, potato and gravy, pie, cake and sauce, which brings croup, scarlet fever, diphtheria and nearly all diseases incident to children. Women suffer more than men because they follow their natural instincts more and eat the same that children do.

The average man of middle age has no real relish for food, and eats mainly because he knows it is necessary. A vigorous child can relish and eat most anything he is obliged to satisfy hunger and can eat most anything without distress, but unnatural food gradually destroys his vigor and by the time he is middle-aged, just when he should be in his prime and more vigorous than at any previous time, he has no real relish for food and cannot eat things without distress, that agreed with him, so far as he was conscious of, when a child.

Animals are healthy and relish food when aged as well as when young, and are always vigorous and strong until their natural decay and death from old age.

Is there any reason why man, the most noble work of God, should not enjoy health and strength as well as animals? Is it right to suppose that man, who is blessed in every other respect above all created things, should be cursed with disease his entire life; that his life should be one continuous struggle, both consciously and unconsciously, with disease? It is not. God has not made anything imperfect. When man uses the perfect food intended for him, and uses it as is intended he shall, he will be free from disease.

PART FIFTH.

Now consider how food should be prepared. Commence with fruit. That needs no preparation further than what it gets in cultivation. No part should be fermented, nor should it be cooked. That destroys it for the purpose it is intended for, namely: To digest other food. There are both nutritive and digestive properties in it; the nutritive properties are only partly destroyed by cooking; the digestive properties are wholly destroyed. By using natural food and uncooked food man can have perfect digestion, which he can not have in any other way. There is a way for man to tell whether digestion is perfect or not. Every one who has handled a horse is aware that the air that comes from the bowels (commonly called breaking wind) has an odor that is not very disagreeable to smell; instead it is rather pleasant to most people. This betokens perfect digestion. Every one is aware that the same thing in man is more or less disagreeable. This is supposed to be necessarily so. But it is not. When natural food is used and digestion is perfect the odor from the air which is necessary to pass from the bowels is no more disagreeable than the odor from the bowels of a horse. By this odor man can tell whether digestion is perfect or not. Perfect digestion cannot be expected at the commencement of the use of natural food. The system must have time to get over the use of unnatural food. It does not require but little meat, lard, sugar or other unnatural food to frustrate perfect digestion. This is a part of the irrefutable evidence that the system herein demonstrated is the law of creation.

To dry fruit does not destroy it. It is not quite as good, yet will answer if no other can be had. It can be used dry by being careful to chew thoroughly—or it can be soaked in water and then used. The water should be boiled and cooled before it is put on the fruit.

Another objection to cooking fruit is, it can not be restored to its original beauty and flavor.

Next take animal and vegetable food. Flour is generally made into bread via fermentation. That should not be. No food should be fermented. That damages its nutritive properties. makes it unpalatable and causes constipation. If man dispenses with fermented bread until the effect of it is gone from the system, the disagreeable smell and taste of it is evidence that it is not suitable for food (man's sense of smell and taste are for the purpose of discerning what is suitable, and no food should be used that is offensive to them:) and if it is eaten the nervous disorder it causes makes him think that the wonder is not so much that so many die prematurely as that so many survive as long as they do. If bread that is prepared right is dispensed with, no matter how long, it does not cause disorder when used again, instead it is more agreeable than if used every day. Flour should be mixed with cream, or its equivalent in butter and butter-milk. the yolk of eggs, water and soda. By mixing flour with animal food each supplies what the other lacks for construction, nutrition and flavor. Flour can be mixed with butter-milk and the butter used when it is eaten, but that is not the best way, because the butter, when not mixed with flour, retards the action of the digestive organs, and has a tendency to injure the kidneys. When the kidneys are diseased none should be used that way. God does not make one part of the apple tasteless and the other part something to make it relish. It is good all through, and that is the way man should prepare the food that is intended for him to prepare. Sour cream or butter-milk should be used instead of cream of tartar or baking powder. Soda should be used in mixing flour whether the animal food used is sour or not.

There is no harm in using soda. Lye will not do to wash the body with, but when its alkaline properties are neutralized by grease and it is made into soap, it is harmless and better than to wash without it. So if soda is taken alone into the stomach it is hurtful, but when its alkaline properties are neutralized by the oil and acid of animal food, which require the alkaline properties of soda to neutralize what would otherwise be the bad effect of them, it is no longer harmful: instead it makes food smell and taste better than it does without it, and keeps the stomach pure and healthy.

All things should be cooked as soon as mixed. None should be left over until the next meal so as to have it freshly baked. thinking that it is just as well if soda is used to make it sweet. That generates the germ of disease and causes boils.

Pop-corn can be ground and the meal prepared in various ways: or it can be boiled whole. When that is done it should be soaked in water long enough before cooking to make the outside tender.

Tea and coffee are for seasoning water as nutmeg, cinnamon, etc., are for seasoning food. There are two parts to either tea or coffee, one is hurtful, the other is beneficial. In steeping the good goes into the water first, and neither should be allowed to stay in the water any longer than necessary to extract the good. Neither should be so strong that it is not pleasant without cream or sugar. No water should be drank until it has been boiled It can be cooled before using in hot weather, and it is better to let it stand until the lime settles, when it can be poured off before using.

PART SIXTH.

Now consider how food should be used. Man should be careful that he does not suffer for any one kind of food. All are more or less necessary or they would not have been created. It does not follow that as some things cannot be grown in some localities they are not needed there.

Class C forms the part of food for man that grain does for animals. The part of hay that does animals good is the leaf that is on the stalk. It is intended by nature to nourish the stalk when it grows to bear seed. The same kind of food for man is class D, and classes A and B are nearly the same; so near that they all serve the purpose for man that hay does for animals. In class C there is no difference. The part used whether for man or animals is the part that grows. It is curious that while there are a great many kinds of this kind of fruit food, chestnuts, walnuts, almonds, etc., there are only two kinds of vegetables, and so far as known, one kind of animal food. Rice and pop-corn are the kinds of vegetable food. Rice is good for a change once in a while but will not do for the main thing, because it will not give the system sufficient strength to endure hardships. If it is alone made to form this class of vegetable food, the skin and muscles become tender and weak, the skin wears off from the hands very quickly in hard work, and the whole system has a sort of mushroom growth, something like rice itself, which is grown in water to a great extent, and like all things grown in that way, is not very substantial. Rice that grows on upland may not have so bad an effect. Pop-corn has a hardy growth and makes the system solid and strong. It should be used every day. Everybody knows how necessary it is for a horse to have grain in order to have perfect development. It is just as necessary for man to have this class of food, and when he does not, he lacks the same in development that a horse lacks that has no grain.

Pop-corn is used only as a sort of oddity for adults and a pleasing morsel for youths and children at times; and as it is small, and not so easily raised as large corn, that is supposed to be all it is fit for; no one thinks it contains anything necessary or indispensable, yet it does, and is the most valuable grain that grows. There is no substitute for it. Potato can be substituted for flour a great deal better than rice can for this grain. Whatever way it is prepared, the outside is coarse enough to keep the bowels loose, which is so much desired. It has none of the hay-like smell and taste that the whole of wheat has, nor the strong, unnatural taste that oat meal has, and it will not cause sour stomach and nausea as these things will. It makes better broth, soup or porridge, than can be made from anything else; no matter how many things are used. Like flour it can be used in some form at every meal with relish and it gives the system more heart, life and vigor, than any other food.

These qualities place it at the head of all food for man. For that reason and in view of the important part it ought to take in food and commerce in the future, it should have a name of its own and not be called some kind of corn because it grows like corn. Wheat grows like rye, yet it is not called some kind of rye; neither is rye called some kind of wheat, but each has a name which sounds better and is more convenient. The name should be short and simple so as to be easily spelled and pronounced and should be unlike the name of any other thing. The letters k-n-o-r-e placed as they are here, the k being silent, make such a name and by that let it be called.

Since writing the foregoing, evidence has come to light which goes to show that the sweet corn commonly used for green corn belongs in this class (C) of food. If it does it is a valuable kind because it grows larger and consequently is more easily raised than pop-corn, yet possibly it being sweet may make it unsuitable for constant use. If it is cooked by boiling when ripe it must be soaked a long time before cooking in order to have the outside tender.

Buttermilk is about forty per cent of cream and is of more value than butter. While it is impossible to use more than the equal proportion of butter without trouble, more than the equal proportion of buttermilk can be safely used, and it is well for those who work hard to use it that way on account of its value for the muscle and brain. A little goes far and care should be taken not to use enough to cause unnatural thirst, inflammation in the bowels and catarrh, which it will if too much is used. When the kidneys and urinary organs are diseased, no butter should be used. While they are recovering the necessary oil can be furnished to the system by the yolk of eggs, and care should be taken not to use enough of them to prevent recovery. No permanent harm will come if the system does not, for the time being, have all the oil it requires when in a normal state. The digestive properties of buttermilk are nearly equal to fruit.

Potato is so near the nature of flour that it is not necessary every day where flour is used.

It will not do to use cream or butter for the yolk of egg or the yolk of egg for cream or butter, thinking that as they are both of an oily nature one will do as well as the other. The yolk of egg is necessary for the nerves; there is no other food that will answer in its place. By its use the hair becomes soft and lustrous, providing no unnatural food is used.

The difference in the immediate effect on the system, after natural food has been used long enough to clear the system from the effect of unnatural food, between supplying it with oil by using cream and the yolk of egg instead of lard and fat meat is: lard and fat meat cause an unnatural burning sensation throughout the entire system: which cream and the yolk of egg do not. There is the same difference between honey and sugar that there is between cream and lard. Honey has a soothing, exhilirating effect and should be often used. It is liable to distress adults who are weak from the use of unnatural food, but will not cause distress after the system gets over the effect of such food. Care should be taken not to use too much seasoning in either food or drink.

No food should be used to excess. The excessive use of fruit, or tea, or coffee, or cream, or any other thing will cause catarrh, which is the forerunner of all disease and is caused either by the use of unnatural or the excessive use of some kind of natural food, and not by a cold as is generally supposed. Catarrh can be caused by not using enough soda to neutralize the acid, and as too much soda causes constipation and is otherwise injurious, it is necessary to be careful that the soda and acid neutralize each other.

Comparatively little animal food is required, and of the two, more yolk of egg than cream, or its equivalent in butter and buttermilk. More buttermilk than yolk of egg can be used. No fruit or any other kind of food should be used when there is catarrh caused by the excessive use of it. Digestion is not quite as perfect when no fruit is used as when it is: but it is nearly as perfect, if no unnatural food is used, and the system thrives.

The amount of food necessary for one man is no criterion by which to determine the amount necessary for another. A bird dog requires more than a heavy bull dog. The bird dog runs what he eats off, hunting: the bull dog lies down and uses up but little nourishment. Some men with light frame and active brain require more than others with heavy frame and less active brain.

The sense of hunger is not a correct indication of man's necessities. If he fasts forty-eight hours, the sense of hunger departs and the first food is not relished. On the other hand if he eats all he is hungry for at every meal he takes more than the system requires, which makes it necessary to fast. When man finds himself surfeited he can stop eating before his sense of hunger is satisfied. When that is done there is a sense of hunger after eating, but it passes away in a short time and there is no more hunger until the next meal time. There is no harm in eating just before sleep, providing there is need of food. When man is surfeited he sleeps and rests better to fast. But there is no more harm in taking food that is natural to keep from suffering hunger during the night than there is in putting on clothes to keep from suffering cold. On the contrary sleep and rest is better.

In eating, the following rules should be observed: No kind of food should be eaten between meals. No more drink than is necessary to satisfy thirst should be taken at meal time. Food should be moistened and swallowed with gastric juice, of which there is enough when natural food is used. Fruit should form the last part of a meal. When nuts or honey are used they should be used with fruit.

Drink should be surrounded by gastric juice in swallowing: (children and horses do this and the effort of drawing the water slowly into the mouth and surrounding it with juice as it is swallowed causes a noise such as children and horses make in drinking,) then it is not so liable to harm when a great deal is used as is necessary when hard work is done in hot weather. It is not necessary to make this noise so that it sounds disagreeable.

PART SEVENTH.

Now consider the effect of this food: To some it may at first appear to be a sacrifice to give up meat and things made from lard and sugar that are generally considered nice and live on the (what may at first appear to be) simple things of this system and it may seem as though man would get tired of it. Man can use the food created for him during life without getting tired. There are some things added as well as taken away, and there is no sacrifice of variety. It is impossible for man to prepare food that is so attractive, either in looks or taste, out of food that is not intended for him as he can out of food that is. After he has used this food long enough to realize the difference in all its bearings nothing would induce him to change. If he was compelled to he would consider it a great sacrifice: even so far as taste is concerned it would be a sacrifice.

The length of time required to effect a change for the better in people who are sick is wonderfully short. Nature is quick to do its work when it has a chance.

There is no food that will build up the human system so fast and perfect, or sustain it so long and well in hardship. By its use man can endure more heat and cold, and do more work and do it easier than by the use of other food, because he has nothing within himself to contend with. It is the only way to perfect health and physical development.

Nothing can be said that will enable man to comprehend the difference between the toughness, solidity, life, vigor, strength and power of endurance of the entire system, after this food is used long enough to make the system new, and when other food is used. It must be experienced to be realized.

NOTES.

If the hand is burning it is not necessary to take it away from the fire slowly for fear of trouble from a sudden change. So it is not necessary to change to this system gradually.

In commencing this system man should not be deceived into thinking that because he has nothing in him to create unnatural heat and stimulus he has nothing in him to give him strength.

If this system is partially tried it may not appear to have a partial good effect, because the natural food used may appear to cause distress when it is the unnatural food that is used with it that causes it.

Satan is wily and not lacking in devices to keep man down.

"Some fell upon stony places where they had not much earth and forthwith they sprung up because they had no deepness of earth.

"And when the sun was up they were scorched and because they had no root they withered away.

"And some fell among thorns and the thorns sprung up and choked them.

"But others fell into good ground and brought forth fruit, some an hundred-fold, some sixty-fold and some thirty-fold.

"Who hath ears to hear let him hear." Mat. 13, 5-9.

There is one thing that man can not hire done. God alone can give him the grace and courage necessary to practice the self denial and endurance necessary to maintain health and perfect physical organization. The brightest and deepest thoughts and most noble purposes are born during travail over great physical trials. Such thoughts and purposes are not given in idle, evil pursuits.

If this system is not condemned through lack of comprehension nor evil design, it will not be condemned.

APPENDIX.

I have not intended to say anything outside of the subject of food, but am aware of one thing that so much needs to be generally understood that I can not refrain from stating it, and to give it due force, state the incident that caused its development.

A man by the name of Charles was once staying with a friend by the name of James who had a valuable jersey cow that had a caked bag. He doctored her according to directions derived from a book by one of the greatest veterinary surgeons of London, England, to no avail. Charles was working for himself at a window where he could look out and see the cow as she stood in the yard, and his sympathy was excited for her. She constantly grew worse and her suffering seemed to be unendurable. His sympathy was increased by the fact that he had read sometime during the winter that what was considered the most valurble jersey cow in the country had died from the same cause, and it was evident that this cow must die unless she was relieved, of which there seemed to be no hope as the treatment she was receiving was doing no good, besides if it had been possible for veterinary surgeons to effect a cure they would have cured the prize cow, there being no doubt but the best known methods had been employed to save her. The thought of what the cow would suffer before she was relieved by death was unendurable to him and he tried to think of some way to relieve her. Finally a thought came to him. He was in the habit of washing himself once a week in the following way: He would take a pail or a tub large enough to stand in without hurting the feet and put enough hot soft water into it to come up to the ankles, then about a quart of hot soft water that had enough soap dissolved in it to make a strong suds and put it on a chair or a bench by the side of the tub and have two or three gallons of hot hard water ready for use, then stand in the tub and with a sponge and a cloth (the cloth for the eyes, face and ears,) wash himself

all over, the hair on the head included, with the suds, taking
care to have the room warm enough to prevent any disagreeable
chill, then with another sponge and cloth and the hot hard
water, (which is better than soft water for the purpose because it
does it quicker and cleaner,) rinse the suds off, which leaves the
body perfectly clean and is much better than to lie down in
a tub of suds and get up and wipe with a towel which leaves
more or less soap in the pores, which although not as bad as
dirt, is not as well as to have the skin perfectly clean, and as
there is more waste cast off through the hands and feet than
other parts of the body, he washed the feet every night, which
they require as much as the body requires washing once a
week. He had noticed that in handling the suds that if there
were any sores or cracks in the hands the inflammation was taken
out, and that it appeared to draw the substance out of the
fingers, and had noticed that the fingers of women after they
had washed clothes were shrunken, and it seemed to him that
if suds had such an effect in so short a time, that possibly by
long continuing it might draw the soreness out of the cow, and
he suggested it to his friend, but he scouted the idea of anything so simple amounting to anything and would not try it.
He was a man of exalted ideas and scorned any trifling; he employed the best in the world in such cases, and if they failed he
calmly submitted to what appeared to him to be inevitable.
While Charles was as careful as his friend and would do noth'ng
from which there was a possibility of harm coming, he was ready
to try anything that appeared reasonable when all other things
had failed. His work was so pressing that he could not leave it
to try the experiment himself, so he had to content himself with
saying what he could to induce his friend to try it. It run along
so until his hurrying job was done and the crisis with the cow
had come. It was evident that she could not hold out much
longer. Her bag was as red as fire and she was in agony. Then
he put two kettles of water on the stove, about seven o'clock in
the evening, and cut enough soap into them to make a strong
suds, and when they got hot took one to the barn and set it
under the cow so that the suds would run back into it and
commenced. Her bag was so sore that she would not allow it to
be touched at first, so he commenced away from it and worked
gradually down to it. When one kettle of water got cold it was
changed for the hot one and the water was kept as hot as it

could be handled. It was a slow job and required care and patience, but by four o'clock the next morning there was no inflammation or cake in the bag, and he had the satisfaction of going to bed with the consciousness that he had relieved the cow from suffering and death. He had quite a severe cold when he commenced, and it was a cold raw windy night in March, but the next day his cold was gone; handling the hot suds had drawn it out.

Where there is soreness or inflammation in man or beast apply hot suds and rub and knead the parts as much as can be endured until there is relief. The suds should not be strong enough to make the skin smart.

There is another thing which, although not established beyond doubt, is of so much interest and importance that it should be investigated and proven, and if it shall not prove to be the cause of and remedy for the diseases named, it is the cause of unthriftiness and trouble and should be understood.

In the fall of 1889 I had five shoats. They were about seven months old and had had the best of care. They throve quite well during the summer, but in the fall they did not thrive and some of them began to act and appear as I had been told hogs act and appear when they are first taken with cholera. Finally they got so bad that there was no question about their being unwell, and everything seemed to indicate that cholera was the cause. As I was pondering over the probability of losing them a thought came to me I had been in the habit of putting a part of their feed on the ground, and in eating it they ate more or less dirt and possibly that might have something to do with it. So I put all their feed in the trough and arranged it so that they would not be likely to get any out. Then their trouble and unthriftiness ceased and they grew fast. Then I began to investigate to see whether or not this is the cause of hog cholera. I went to a neighbor who had lost about thirty a few years before who gave me the following information: All his hogs had been attacked except two stock hogs that he kept shut up in pens off from the ground. They escaped although the drove of stricken and dying hogs were around the pens all the time and the pens were not so tight but what they could nearly get their noses together in places, but he was afraid that they might sooner or later be attacked from being so much exposed, and took the most valuable one out of his pen and drove him into a yard across the road where in course of time he was attacked and died, but the one that remained in the pen was not attacked and was the only one in the drove that was not. At the time he took pains to investigate it as much as he could and found that wherever hogs were kept in pens off from the ground they escaped, he heard of but one hog that was in a pen that was attacked and died. Could not say whether there was a floor in the pen or not. Had noticed that all farmers on one side of the road that passed his place had lost all their hogs, while the farmers on the other side of the same road had lost none. That the farmers joining him on one side had lost all while the farmers joining him on the other side: (he owned land on both sides of the road,) had lost none. It appeared to go in streaks. He sold one neighbor two sows (of the same breed that he kept,) out of his drove, the spring before. They raised pigs and ran in a lot across the road from and in sight of his hogs, not one of them being attacked, while he lost every hog he had outside of the pen except one old sow. She was attacked but lived through it. He found that everywhere where it raged the youngest, smallest and weakest had been attacked and died first, the largest and strongest escaping to the last. Was not at home when his hogs were first attacked, had gone to Nebraska on a visit or business, and did not get home until a great many were dead. Had been in the habit of feeding the hogs himself when at home and naturally selected a clean place to put the corn. Had never lost any hogs previous to this year. Upon looking back and taking into consideration all the facts and circumstances, he had no doubt but the hogs were fed while he was gone so that they got a great deal of ground mixed with their feed, the one that was across the road in a yard by himself included. Then I went to his neighbor across the road who gave me the following information: He had given his hogs a little kerosene oil and sulphur in their swill as he had noticed that hogs that were attacked had sore throats, and kerosene was good for that and sulphur was good to physic and regulate the bowels: had fed corn on the ground but had selected clean places to put the feed, had always done that in feeding anything. His hogs had run in a lot across the road from his neighbors' which were dying. Then I saw another man who lived about three miles from the first two whose hogs had escaped, although a near neighbor, (who has since moved away,) lost heavily. He said he had done nothing to prevent it: had fed corn on the ground and had always been in the habit of selecting a clean place to feed anything; could not say how his neighbor who lost hogs fed.

There has been no hog cholera since and this is as far as I have been able to carry the investigation. Following is the sum so far as gone: 1. No hogs that have been known (the pen where the hog that was shut up died may not have had a floor and may have been fed on the ground) to have been shut up so that they could not get the feed mixed with ground have been attacked, although in the case of the stock hogs referred to, they were surrounded by hogs that were constantly dying from the disease and the pens were such that the hogs could nearly get their noses together in places in smelling each other. The hog that was taken out of the pen and away from the stricken hogs and fed on the ground in the same way that the drove was, was attacked and died. 2. No hogs have been known to have been attacked when fed on the ground when pains has been taken to feed in a clean place, although in the case of the second farmer referred to they were of the same breed as those that were dying from the disease, and the two droves ran in lots that had only a road to separate them. 3. There is no hog cholera in the eastern states where farmers are in the habit of feeding in a trough, it rages only in the western states where farmers are in the habit of feeding on the ground. 4. Numbers make no difference. The one stock hog in the yard alone was attacked although on the same side of the road and within one hundred rods of the drove that escaped. 5. The cause of the youngest, smallest and weakest being attacked and dying first may be that the largest and strongest drive them away and get the cleanest corn which preserves them to the last. There is a great deal of difference in ground, and it is impossible for hogs to get as much ground mixed with feed on some farms, even though there is no pains taken in feeding, as on others, which may be another reason why some droves escape. The reason why the disease has not raged as hard for the last few years as it did, may be that farmers who had been losing steadily suddenly gave up the business, there being no perceptible falling off in the supply because those who had lost hogs had had none to sell. The following may be the history and origin of the disease: When farmers first came west they were in limited circumstances. The country was undeveloped and but few hogs were raised, which were fed in troughs according to the eastern custom, but as the country developed and great crops of corn and large droves of hogs were raised and labor was scarce and wages were high, hogs were fed on the ground because of the time and expense saved, which resulted in producing the disease.

The foregoing facts and indications are sufficient to justify those who are interested in investigating, experimenting and proving whether this is the cause of the disease or not.

Whether it is or not there is one thing sure, disease and unthriftiness to a greater or less extent come from feeding so that ground and dirt gets mixed with the feed.

I bought and kept the pigs for the purpose of experimenting with food on them. Following is the result of the experiment: 1. While they eat and appear to like apples as they eat and appear to like anything when they are hungry, they are not necessary as an aid in digestion, (as they are in man,) nor necessary for their perfect thriftiness and development. 2. The essential thing in their perfect thriftiness and development is that their food shall be soured but not fermented before it is given to them. They are created to like soured (not sour like sour apples,) things, a sort of garbage cleaner, as buzzards are created to like the flesh of dead animals after it is decayed. If fed before the feed is soured let the feed be the best that can be had for them. They will eat but little and grow slow and appear stunted and lifeless and the tails will hang straight and limp, but if the same feed is soured (not fermented,) before they are fed, they will eat heartily and grow fast, and their tails will curl clear up to the body and they will be as sleek as moles and full of life and vigor. It may be well to say for the benefit of those who are not accustomed to pigs, that those who are, consider a curly tail a sign of thrift.

For reasons given elsewhere, all animals should have grain. Every one accustomed to using horses is aware that they will do enough more work by having grain than to more than pay the expense of it. The work of cows is to produce milk and they will produce enough more by having grain than to more than pay for it. Growth in young animals is what work is in old ones and they need the same nourishment. It is impossible for anything to have the utmost vigor and thriftiness so long as something essential to its perfect organization is lacking.

It is strange that hogs are created so that they do not require salt, (a very little can be mixed in their food without any appear-

ance of trouble, but they will not touch it of their accord,) while
all other domestic animals do and can not thrive without it. A
few years ago one of my neighbors had a fine cow. In the spring
after she was turned to grass she did not look well. Her hair
was harsh, her eyes were dull and she appeared lifeless. I won-
dered what ailed her. She had had the best of feed and a warm
stable all winter and was in good grass then, and there was no
reason why she should not be as lively as ever. She was naturally lively, bright eyed, and hearty. Finally it occured to me
that it might be want of salt: the neighbor trusted her care to his
boys who may not have salted her. So I told him what I had
been thinking. He brought some salt and as soon as she saw
him with it she rushed across the yard toward him, and when he
threw it down ate it in one-quarter of the time that it generally
takes a cow to eat salt and stood longing for more, although she
had had twice as much as a cow generally eats. He thought she
had better not have more then, but he saw that she had it three
times a week after that, and in a short time her old life and vigor
returned.

No salt should be mixed in the food of any kind of animals.
No kind will eat more or less than they require if it is kept where
they can help themselves when they want it. There is a great
deal of difference in the amount required by each kind of animals.
Cattle require more than horses, and hens require but little, yet
they need what they require as bad as animals that require
more. It does not take much mixed in the food of hens to cause
disease and death.

The question arises if unnatural food is the cause of consumption in man what is the cause of consumption in animals. The
answer is the same cause.

All food that is natural for animals is created so that no stalk
can serve two purposes perfectly. The seed of stalks that are
intended for hay or fodder is not suitable for grain. The stalks
that produce grain are not suitable for hay or fodder. There is
one thing that comes nearer being an exception to this rule than
any other, that is corn. Corn stalks makes good fodder for cattle and corn makes good grain, yet neither is perfect. The
stalks, because they have lost too much of their nutritive power
in nourishing the grain, the grain because it is too heating. If
cattle are to be fed for the purpose of putting on fat corn is good
feed, but to put on fat is not the purpose for which cattle are

intended nor the purpose for which they should be fed. The primary purpose for which they are intended is to produce milk, and that is the purpose for which they should be fed, and for that purpose there are other grains that are better, which shows that corn is an imperfect grain, which with the fact that there is no better fodder for cattle (each kind of animals has its peculiar liking for some particular kind of fodder and grain and will thrive better on that than on any other kind, which kind of stalks and grain is best adapted to each kind of animals is not yet fully known,) if it is used when it contains the greatest amount of nourishment shows that corn is hardly an exception to the rule.

If animals can not thrive on the seed of things that are intended for fodder or hay, it is impossible for them to use the seed of things of which no part is intended for food without trouble. No part of flax or cotton are intended for food, and it is the use of a part of these unnatural things (sometimes molasses and other unnatural things are used) which is the cause of consumption in cattle.

In regard to disease in cattle known as Texas fever. Animals are created so that there are certain elements necessary for the formation of perfect blood, and consequent perfect organization of the system, and when one of these elements is lacking there is imperfect blood and consequent imperfect organization of the system with weakness if not disease. One of the elements necessary for perfect blood in cattle is salt, (hogs are created so that salt is not necessary to form perfect blood for them,) and cattle are allowed to run year after year on the southern plain without it, which must cause weakness and trouble, but whether it goes far enough to cause Texas fever or not is a question. In talking with some pioneer farmers about it some of them said: "Salt is not necessary for cattle. They have got in the habit of liking it from its being given to them for generations, but they are just as well off without it. When this country was first settled the people were too poor to buy salt for cattle and they did not have any to amount to anything. One of them said: "Thinking about it puts me in mind of something that I saw once that I never shall forget. A steer that had run all summer in the woods without salt was brought up in the fall and given a handfull and I never saw anything eat anything as the steer ate that salt. He dug a hole in the ground and ate it to get every grain there was." Animals do not acquire habits unless taught by man. They are created with an instinct that tells them what is, and what is not, necessary for their perfect organization, and if left to their own accord will not eat anything that is not, nor go without anything that is, necessary for their perfect organization.

There is another thing that possibly may have something to do with this disease. Domestic animals may not thrive as well on the wild grass of the plains as buffalos and other wild animals which it is natural for. Animals that are created for tame domestic animals may require tame grass. Experiments may prove that these and possibly other similar things are the cause of this disease instead of its being caused by the cattle being infected by the animals that are on the surface of the ground that are supposed to be the cause of this supposed to be infectious disease.

To the Average Man of Mature Mind:

Read and study the book until it is thoroughly understood, then if you are so tied to the fashions and customs of the age that you cannot test it now, put it away until you are sick. Then after the doctors' kind and benevolent manners, soothing and encouraging words and beneficient and sanitary regulations (the most talented and concientious of the profession say that so far as drugs are concerned the science of medicine is a failure. Sir Astley Cooper the most celebrated English practicioner of his age said, "On the whole, more harm than good is done by medication." Professor Brousais, who was styled the illustrious professor of Valdi Grace, said, "I agree that medicine has rendered to suffering man the service of offering consolation by ever fostering chimerical hopes, but such service is far from placing it on a level with other natural sciences. It rather seems to class it with astrology, superstition and all kinds of quackery." Professor Magendie, whose writings are in the libraries of nearly all physicians, says, "It is especially where medicine is most active that mortality is greatest." Similar statements have been made by a great many others of high standing in the profession. These statements have been proven to be true by experiments made in hospitals where repeated experiments on large numbers with different diseases showed that of those who received medicine a larger per cent. died than of those who received no medicine, and that those who received medicine and recovered were longer in doing so than those who received no medicine) fail to effect a cure, test this system and if you are not too far gone you will recover. One such experience is enough for a wise man. If you cannot recover call your children around you and tell them that notwithstanding you have done everything you could to promote health, life is a failure—It is ended long before nature has run its course and that you must leave them forever, so far as this world is concerned, prematurely and unexpectedly. And advise them to try to avoid a similar fate by trying some other way.

Very respectfully and deferentially submitted by

THE AUTHOR.